Kirk and the See-Through Specs

Space Base gave Kirk some
See-Through Specs.
The See-Through Specs
could see through things.

Joe tried the See-Through Specs on Kirk.

Joe could see Kirk's pants but he did not tell Kirk.

THE LAST LAUGH

Contents

Stories illustrated by Chris Garbutt and Frances Castle

In this story

 Kirk, a Space Cop

 Joe, a Space Cadet

 Zorgon, their enemy

Tricky words

- Space Base
- See-Through Specs
- tried
- radar
- steal
- use
- wait

 Introduce these tricky words and help the reader when they come across them later!

Story starter

Commander Kirk is a Space Cop travelling across Space in his starship. Joe, a Space Cadet, is on board too. Kirk and Joe battle against their evil enemy, Zorgon. Space Base has just sent Kirk their latest invention – See-Through Specs that could see through things.

Then Kirk looked at the radar. "Zorgon is coming," he said. "He is coming to steal the See-Through Specs."

"Sir," said Joe, "I have a plan. I will use the See-Through Specs to stop Zorgon."

"How will the See-Through Specs stop Zorgon?" said Kirk.

"Wait and see," said Joe.

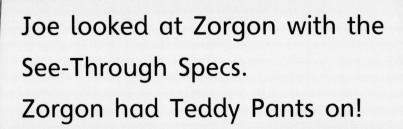

Joe looked at Zorgon with the
See-Through Specs.
Zorgon had Teddy Pants on!

"Look, sir," said Joe, "Zorgon
has Teddy Pants on."
Kirk looked through the
See-Through Specs.

"Ha! Ha! Ha!" said Kirk to Zorgon.
"You have Teddy Pants on!"
Kirk and Joe laughed and laughed
at Zorgon.

Zorgon went very red.
"Just you wait," he said.
"I will be back!"

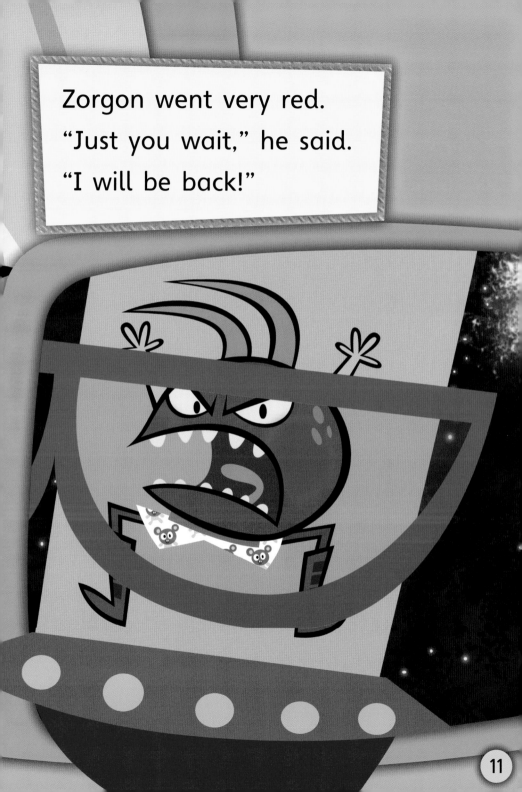

Then Kirk tried the See-Through Specs on Joe. And it was Joe's turn to go red!

Text Detective

- Why did Zorgon go very red?
- Why did Joe say "Wait and see"?
- What do you think Kirk said to Joe at the end?

Word Detective

- **Phonic Assessment:** Initial consonant clusters

  Listen to the word 'plan'. Can you blend the two phonemes at the beginning of the word? Write the word.

- Listen to the word 'stop'. Can you blend the two phonemes at the beginning of the word? Write the word.

- Listen to the word 'tried'. Can you blend the two phonemes at the beginning of the word? Write the word.

Super Speller

Can you spell these words from memory?

things   said   wait

HA! **HA!** **HA!**

Q Who flies through the air in his underwear?

A Peter Pants!

In this story

 Max

 Tom

Tricky words

- tarantula
- pencil case
- laughed
- scorpion
- vampire
- camera
- picture

Introduce these tricky words and help the reader when they come across them later!

Story starter

Max likes to play jokes on people. Each week he spends his pocket money at the joke shop. One day at school Max put his joke tarantula in Tom's pencil case. But Tom didn't laugh. He was fed up with Max's jokes.

Max and the Best Joke Ever

Max put his joke tarantula in
Tom's pencil case.
Max laughed a lot.
But Tom didn't laugh.
He was fed up with Max's jokes.

Then at lunch time, Max got a shock.
There was a big scorpion in his lunch box!

"I put that joke scorpion in your lunch box!" said Tom.
Tom laughed a lot.

But Max didn't laugh.
He didn't like Tom's joke at all.

Then at football time,
Max got a shock.
There was a vampire bat
in his bag!

"I put that joke bat in your bag!"
said Tom.
Tom laughed a lot.

But Max didn't laugh.
He was fed up with Tom's jokes.

19

On the way home, Max looked in the joke shop. He saw a joke camera.

"That camera is just what I need to play a joke on Tom!" said Max. He went into the shop.

The next day at school, Max said to Tom,
"No more jokes, OK?"
"OK!" said Tom.

"I will just take your picture," said Max.

Max took Tom's picture.
Tom got wet!
Max laughed and laughed.
"That was my best joke *ever*!"
said Max.

Quiz

Text Detective

- Why did Max buy the joke camera?
- Why didn't Max laugh when Tom put the joke bat in his bag?
- Do you like to play practical jokes? Do you laugh when someone plays a joke on you?

Word Detective

- **Phonic Assessment:** Final consonant clusters

  Listen to the word 'just'. Can you blend the two phonemes at the end of the word? Write the word.
- Listen to the word 'went'. Can you blend the two phonemes at the end of the word? Write the word.
- Listen to the word 'lunch'. Can you blend the two phonemes at the end of the word? Write the word.

Super Speller

Can you spell these words from memory?

didn't   looked   ever

HA! HA! HA!

Q Why don't vampire bats live alone?

A They like to hang out with their friends!